Tune IN THE MIND

—JAP GAYATRI—

by

Swami Chinmayananda

Central Chinmaya Mission Trust

Printed upto December 2004 to November 2011 - 35,000 copies
Revised Edition - February 2014 - September 2023 - 12,350 copies
Reprint - February 2025 - 3,000 copies

Published by:
Chinmaya Prakashan
The Publications Division of
Central Chinmaya Mission Trust
Sandeepany Sadhanalaya
Saki Vihar Road, Mumbai 400072, India
Tel.: +91-22-2803 4900
Email: ccmtpublications@chinmayamission.com
Website: www.chinmayamission.com

Distribution Centre in the USA:
Chinmaya Publications West
560 Bridgetown Pike
Feasterville, PA 19053-7240, USA
Tel.: (215) 396-0390, Fax: (215) 396-9710
Email: publications@chinmayamission.org
Website: www.chinmayapublications.com

Designed by: Chinmaya Kalpanam, Mumbai

Printed by: Usha Multigraphs Pvt. Ltd., Mumbai

ISBN 978-81-7597-628-3

Preface

This book contains Śāṅkara bhāṣya on Gāyatrī mantra on page 29 to 39, Considering the fact that Gāyatrī mantra is the king of mantras and Śāṅkara bhāṣya is the most authoritative and accepted commentary wherever available in this edition, we have added transliteration as well as word meaning to the bhāṣya. We do hope that the sincere spiritual seekers would find it more useful.

Diacritical marks are used for transliteration of Sanskrit words in the commentary. The English plural sign 's' has been added to untranslated Sanskrit words. A key to the transliteration and pronunciation has been added in the beginning of the book.

Publishers

Transliteration and Pronunciation Guide

In this book, Devanagari characters are transliterated according to the scheme adopted by the International Congress of Orientalists at Athens in 1912. In it one fixed pronunciation value is given to each letter; f, q, w, x and z are not called to use. According to this scheme:

Devanagari	Translit-eration	Sounds Like	Devanagari	Translit-eration	Sounds Like
अ	a	son	ढ्	ḍh	adhesive*
आ	ā	father	ण्	ṇ	under*
इ	i	different	त्	t	tabla
ई	ī	feel	थ्	th	thumb
उ	u	full	द्	d	this
ऊ	ū	boot	ध्	dh	Gandhi
ऋ	ṛ	rhythm*	न्	n	nose
ॠ	ṝ	**	प्	p	pen
ऌ	ḷ	**	फ्	ph	phantom*
ए	e	evade	ब्	b	boil
ऐ	ai	delight	भ्	bh	abhor
ओ	o	core	म्	m	mind
औ	au	now	य्	y	yes
क्	k	calm	र्	r	right
ख्	kh	khan	ल्	l	love
ग्	g	gate	व्	v	very
घ्	gh	ghost	श्	ś	shut
ङ्	ṅ	ankle*	ष्	ṣ	sugar
च्	c	chuckle	स्	s	simple
छ्	ch	witch*	ह्	h	happy
ज्	j	justice	ं	ṁ	improvise
झ्	jh	Jhansi	ः	ḥ	**
ञ्	ñ	banyan	क्ष्	kṣ	action
ट्	ṭ	tank	त्र्	tr	three*
ठ्	ṭh	**	ज्ञ्	jñ	gnosis
ड्	ḍ	dog	ऽ	’	a silent ‘a’

* These letters don’t have an exact English equivalent. An approximation is given here.

** These sounds cannot be approximated in English words.

Contents

Japa Yoga

You may wonder why a student of Vedānta listening to and reflecting upon discourses on the upaniṣads and the *Gītā* should care to take up any method of sādhanā other than pure meditation. It is natural for seekers in their blind enthusiasm to come to question the importance of japa for a seeker of the Self. This doubt comes out of a confusion in the understanding of the japa yoga.

Japa is a training by which the ever dancing rays of the mind are compelled to behave in some order and rhythm and thereby bring out, of their co-operative effort, a single melody of repeated mantra chanting.

In this practising, the mind becomes extremely single pointed. In fact, japa properly done can more effectively bring about a sustained single pointedness than all the hasty methods of meditation. A mind seasoned with japa is like tinned food which gets ready for consumption after a few seconds' warming up on the fire. A short period of meditation can take a japa prepared mind to unimaginable heights in an impossibly short time.

Japa is a training for the mind in fixing itself to a single line of thinking. We cannot pronounce a word without a thought form rising up immediately in us; nor can we have a thought form without its corresponding name. Try! Can you repeat the word 'pen' without its form? Can you? In this close connection between the name and the form lies the underlying principle in the technique of japa.

Again, love is not generated where sufficient thought is not bestowed. You love your near and dear relatives more than your uncle's sister-in-law's nephew, whom probably you had seen and even admired; yet, love is not there, for you have not spent sufficient thought over that child. Thus, japa in a prayer room performed in all intensity, and training oneself to repeat mentally His names constantly during the wakeful hours, are the sure ways of developing devotion (bhakti). It is always the repetition of thinking that brings about the fastness in all attachments. The less one thinks of a thing, the less one gets attached to it. The opposite is also equally true: the more one thinks of a thing the more one gets attached to it.

The supreme reality is experienced through meditation alone. But the boat to reach the goal, namely, meditation, is rigged with the practice of devotion through japa. In meditation one is wingless if one has not acquired a decent share of concentration-power and a perfect knowledge of how to fix one's mind at will, at a single point, for some length of time. Meditation is keeping the mind hitched on to one line of thought, to the complete exclusion of all other dissimilar thought currents. To succeed in this, we must learn to stop at will all other dissimilar thought currents. This mental capacity is gained through japa when intelligently practised along with a regulation of the normal life lived.

Japa is a very effective mental discipline for spiritual progress. In recent history there is the instance of the esteemed teacher of Śivājī, Samartha Rāmadāsa, who perfected himself through the japa yoga of the Śrī Rāma mantra:

'Śrī Rāma Jaya Rāma Jaya Jaya Rāma'. Bhagavān Yogeśvara Kṛṣṇa Himself says in the *Gītā*: 'I am, among the yogas, the japa yoga.'

'How must I start?' To do japa is the way to perform the japa yoga. What happened to that holiday maker who waited on the seashore for the waves to subside so that he may take his bath comfortably? Don't waste your time in vain on the shores of life; get into the ocean of this bliss and be refreshed.

Have a special room for your prayers; fix a charming picture of your heart's Lord, at such a height from the floor that when you sit in front of it, the Lord's feet shall be in level with your eyes. Spread a plain seat (āsana) in front of your iṣṭa, the Lord of your heart. Have a mālā (rosary) of 108 beads. Now start the japa, behind closed doors please, to begin with. Sitting on the āsana in any comfortable, legs-folded pose, in the beginning, gaze at the Lord's beaming face, body, legs, feet. Now slowly raise the gaze up from feet, legs and body, to the face of the Lord. Close the eyes now; feel His presence within you and try to visualise the Lord exactly as in the picture. This visualisation of the

Lord should be done within you in your love heart, which is exactly on the right side of the physical heart. This is the spiritual heart centre where, if you meditate, your success is doubly assured. Feel.....feel His presence.

Now repeat your iṣṭa mantra a few times, slowly, steadily with all the love you are capable of. This invokes the devotion (bhakti) in you to do japa most effectively. Take the mālā; search for the off bead: this is called the Meru. Bring the tips of your ring finger and thumb together, and let the mālā be hung at this junction, repeat fervently your iṣṭa mantra; at each repetition turn one bead with the middle finger, always allowing the index finger to stand apart.

The index finger is considered to be an 'outcast' because of its language. This finger is generally used in pointing out the 'other', in accusing 'another', in threatening and so on. Essentially the index finger is used to express duality and the otherness of things and beings!!

When you have thus repeated 108 times your chosen mantra, naturally, you will come back to the meru bead: you have now done one mālā. Now be careful: don't cross the meru; turn the mālā in such a way that the 109th mantra is counted on the bead with which the 107th mantra was registered. Thereafter proceed in all sincerity and finish with your second mālā of japa. Thus do 20 mālās of japa twice a day... once in the morning and once in the evening.

A mantra is a word symbol or symbols representing and expressing, as nearly as possible, the particular view of God and the universe they stand for. There is nothing secret about these mantras. All of them are in the scriptures, but when the mantra is given to the disciple by an illumined teacher, it becomes a living seed. The teacher, by his spiritual power, gives life to the word, and at the same time awakens the spiritual powers latent .in the disciple. That is the secret of the teacher's initiation.

Just as a 'mantra' is an aid to meditation, worship of Kālī, Durgā, and so on is also an aid to meditation. The latter is called worship of God through a 'pratīka' or a 'pratimā'. Mind you, it is not the 'pratīka' or the 'pratimā' that is worshipped, but the God in the 'pratīka' or 'pratima'. The 'pratīka' or 'pratimā' stands only as a suggestion thereof.

These various forms of worship have been provided to suit the needs of different types of men at different stages of their spiritual evolution. This is just like a man who when he begins to learn writing, first draws big scrawls, before he can successfully try a smaller hand. So too a person must acquire the power of concentrating his thoughts by fixing the mind first upon divine forms, and then after a fair success therein, by fixing it upon the formless divine.

Start today, right now! There is no moment more sacred or so auspicious as here and now for spiritual practice. Japa is an easy method for men like us, kicked about and bullied by the worlds without and within.

(a) **Mantras fromVedānta:**

Tat Tvam Asi – That thou art;

Aham Brahma Asmi – I am Brahman;

Ayam Ātmā Brahma – This Self is Brahman;

Śivo'ham Śivo'ham – I am Śiva – auspiciousness;

Tadeva Satyam Tat Brahma – That alone is the Truth – that is Brahman;

Ānando'ham Ānando'ham – I am ānanda, I am bliss;

Haṁsaḥ So'ham, So'ham Haṁsaḥ – I am He, He is me;

He is me, I am He.

Or

(b) Mantras from Purāṇa :

Om Namo Nārāyaṇāya;

Om Śrī Rāma Jaya Rāma Jaya Jaya Rāma;

Om Namaḥ Śivāya;

Om Śrī Śāṇmukhāya Namaḥ;

Om Śrī Rāmacandrāya Namaḥ;

Om Śrī Lakṣmyai Namaḥ, and so on.

Anyone of the above mantras can be taken up according to taste, faith and devotion for the purpose of regular, purposeful, intense chanting.

While doing japa remember that even though the āsana, the beads rolling, the iṣṭa devatā and such other equipments for japa are external, japa in itself is not physical but it is mental, and is to be raised to a still deeper level. What I mean is that neither a mere rolling of the beads nor a non-stop muttering in the mouth can constitute the japa yoga.

It should be an all out intense and sincere effort of the japist to bring forth from his mind and intellect all the possible faculties...like emotion, discrimination, sensitiveness, will, logic, reason, sympathy, love, faith and so on...and pour them all into the act of concentrating upon 'mental chanting' of the sacred mantra, performed at the feet of the Lord's form, which is visualised steadily within the naked chamber of the bosom.

Japa generally enchants the unwary practitioner into the jungles of unproductive thought wanderings. If the student is not diligent enough to detect it and arrest the flow of thoughts, it is possible that his japa lands him in a dark ditch of frustration and stupor.

This warning is to be strictly given; many of the japists we see today in India – why, we can say, all over the world in all creeds – have to a large extent rendered themselves pervert, and strangely enough we find that the ugliness of their psychological beauty is directly proportional to the amount of japa they have practised!!

To begin with, this seemingly simple yoga should not be overpractised. Start with one mālā of japa a day, slowly raise the number of mālās. You may start by increasing the number of mālās at first on convenient holidays only, and when you are convinced of your mental capacity to sustain your inspired attention for the required period of time, then alone should you take to long sittings at japa.

Another difficulty that comes to japists, and this is common to ninety per cent of them, is an irresistible attack of sleep while doing japa and a shamelessly evident tendency to express bad temper soon after japa sādhanā. The seeker should not get annoyed at himself on these observations. He should learn to patiently fight these tendencies and win them over.

Sleep comes because a mind in japa is a mind at rest. Train the mind not to sleep in the salubrious climate within. It is natural for children to sleep in a running car and the poor thing gains no thrill of the trip.

Bad temper comes because of two reasons: suppression of tendencies and fatigue. The former starts with the japist's annoyance at his mind wandering here and there during his japa. The latter is caused by exhaustion, because to hold the mind in balance at a given line of thought is a great strain to the beginner and, therefore, his mind gets fatigued.

A new driver at the wheel knows not how to relax, and thus, he unnecessarily exhausts himself before he has driven around the next corner of his own street. A new swimmer will be fatiguing himself within a few yards; a new housewife gets tired of looking after her very firstborn. Later on, the very same woman easily manages her half a dozen, along with her late cousin's four little kids....and yet, discovers for herself plenty of spare time and mental ease for her afternoon chats with the neighbours.

There is an art of economising energy in work. There is for every work, its own required stamina to be drawn from our individual personality. This is equally true in all spiritual activities called yogas. One's subtle judgment upon the works of an artist – as distinct from those of another – is not a detail which is really taught, but it is that which, during practice, one comes to discover for oneself. The same rule applies in the art of yoga also. The artistic rhythm and harmony of any yoga will have to be discovered by the practitioner all for himself. This will come as a result of continuous practice in the right direction.

A japist's attempt is always to maintain his mind in one fixed line of divine thinking. To one who has gained a sufficient poise in this subjective art of single pointedness gained through the practice of contemplation, to him, meditation is natural, for, meditation itself is but a conscious attempt to 'maintain' the mind in one channel of thoughts belonging to the same species.

Japa is, thus, a very healthy and effective aid to meditation, if properly practised and regularly pursued.

Regularity and sincerity are the secrets of success in spirituality. Guard the mind against all excesses and make it immune to selfishness and passion. Watch how imperceptibly the mind ties itself down with things and beings, happenings and circumstances by its own unintelligent attachments. Even when all these warnings are faithfully obeyed, there is still a subtle danger of the japa activity being muddled with our incorrigible thirst for fruits. Profit motive is the strongest urge in man in all his strenuous activities. Japa, polluted by this profit motive (sa-kāma}, cannot end in the spiritual effulgence of the one doing it.

Consider the japa activity as a yajña. Gather the purest and the best that you can eke out from yourself and offer them all into the japa as devoted oblations. The potential strength of blessing that lies dormant in japa will thereby be invoked, and to one who is under its grace, meditation is homecoming, after a pleasant and joyous ride through sunny fields and flowery gardens.

The effectiveness of japa, to a large extent, depends upon the spirit of surrender with which the seeker is practising it. This idea of surrender should not be merely an emotional explosion of a sentimental make belief. It should be a solid act of understanding, at once deliberate and conscious. When once we understand the principle behind the surrender, we shall discover the bridge that connects the pasture lands of bhakti and the snowy peaks of jñāna.

Let us, for example take a typical mantra and try to discover the attitude of surrender implied in it – Om Namo Nārāyaṇāya: 'My prostrations unto Nārāyaṇa.' Prostration is not merely a physical act of bowing but it is a conscious act of discovering the greater in us and seeking our identity with it. To tune ourselves with the better or the nobler, and thereby gathering unto ourselves the very qualities and greatness of the Higher, is true prostration.

In order to prostrate there must be, at least, two factors: the lesser that prostrates and the Higher at whose feet the prostration is offered. Within each one of us, there is the matter-conditioned ego and the unconditioned eternal Self. The japist in himself is trying to end his false ego at the altar of himself – the supremely divine

Self, Śrī Nārāyaṇa. Thus, during the japa the individual practising it will be sincerely striving to surrender totally his personality to Nārāyaṇa who is his concept of the reality.

Thus, a mantra is but a formula that explains to us, at once, not only what is the enduring Truth in life but also the technique by which we can reach it. Om is the symbol of the infinite which is finally attained through surrender (namaḥ) of all our false identifications with the matter envelopments at the feet of the 'the core of things' – Nārāyaṇa. When from ourselves, our individual personality concept is removed, we come to experience the Nārāyaṇa-tattva in ourselves which, being the same everywhere at all times, is Itself the experience of Om, the Brahman.

In fact, it is evident now that japa properly undertaken is not only a preparation for meditative flights but it can in itself serve as a vehicle which can lift us, from the pains and ugliness of our imperfections, to the very throne of the infinite, the perfect.

May you come to realise the joy and bliss of this supreme sādhanā – the japa yoga.

Mantra and Japa – Gāyatrī

Mantras are given out by the seers. Ṛṣis are the 'seers' of the mantras – meaning, they are the Men of Wisdom who had realised the deep significances and the pregnant imports of the mantras. Every mantra has a presiding deity. The belief is that when one chants a mantra he is to do so keeping in his mind the form of the deity – then like one being called by one's own name answers to it readily, so too here the devatā is invoked easily. That is the faith. It is also the belief that on chanting any mantra for ten thousand times alone can we hope to see any benign influence of the japa on ourselves. Whenever japa is undertaken, the form of the devatā is to be maintained in front of the mind's eye. To facilitate this we have a meditation stanza (dhyāna śloka) that describes the devatā associated with every mantra.

Some insist upon the ritualistic formalities, prescribed in the upāsanā section of the Vedas as unavoidable. The orthodox believe that, as the japa numbers mount up higher and higher, homa, tarpaṇa, large-scale feeding and such other sacred acts are to be performed as limbs of the japa yoga. This view is not universally accepted as there is yet another powerful school who believe that sincerity and faith are the very core of the japa sādhanā, and any one with a chaste heart of love can faithfully do his japa. He needs no such formal and ritualistic entanglements to fulfil his sacred vow.

There are three types of mantras: those that invoke the low powers of nature (tāmasika); those that excite and manifest might and power (rājasika); and lastly, those that lead to spiritual experience (sāttvika).

All those mantras again fall under two classifications: (a) those that need to be only chanted and there is no need for one to know their meaning; and (b) those mantras that are of the nature of an invocation and the devotee must necessarily know the meaning of those mantras without which he will not be able to bring his mind to play upon the divine theme constantly.

The Vaidika mantras are both in poetry and in prose; the metrical mantras are called the 'ṛk' and the prose mantras are called the 'yajus'.

Of all the mantras the most powerful and the significant one is the single syllabled incantation called the praṇava. This is the Om.

The available literature upon the significance of this Vaidika mantra is almost voluminous. Nowhere in this world can we meet with a more sacred symbol that has got such a vast amount of significance.

From Vaidika times until the present day, the word Om has been taken as a symbol and as an aid to meditation by spiritual aspirants. It is accepted both as one with Brahman and as the medium, the logo, connecting man and God. The entire history of the syllable· is in the revelations of the Vedas and in the declarations of the Upaniṣads.

There is a verse in the Vedas: 'prajāpatir-vai idam agra āsīt' (In the beginning was prajāpati, the Brahman); 'Tasya vāk-dvitīya āsīt' (With whom was the word)[1]; 'Vāg-vai paramam Brahma' (And the word was verily the supreme

[1] The idea belongs· to Hinduism and in the fourth Gospel of the New Testament we read it repeated: 'In the beginning was the word and the word was with God and the word was God'.

Brahman). This sphoṭa has its symbol in the word Om. Thus, in the *Maitrayāṇa-upaniṣad* after it has been said that there is one Brahman without words and a second, a Word Brahman, we are told that the word is the syllable Om. The sound of Om is also called praṇava meaning that it is something that pervades life, or runs through prāṇa or breath.

The very central theme of *Māṇḍūkya-upaniṣad* is the syllable Om through which the mystery of Brahman is gathered to a point. The text of this Upaniṣad first treats Om in terms of the doctrine of Upaniṣad of the three states of waking, dream and deep sleep, but then passes on to the 'fourth' (turīya), thus transporting us beyond the typical sphere of Upaniṣad into that of the later 'classic advaita-vedānta.' Speaking of Om, *Taittirīya-upaniṣad* says: 'Thou art the sheath of Brahman,' that is, Om is the container for the Supreme and, therefore, invoking Om is invoking the Supreme.

In every piece of music, there are three aspects, viz, (1) the meaning of the song, (2) The laws of music, and (3) the sound of the song.

Similarly, in Om, there are three aspects. The first is the mere sound that is the mere mantra as pronounced by the mouth; the second is the meaning of the syllable, which is to be realised through feeling; and the third is the application of 'Om' to your character, singing it in your acts and so through your life.

'Om' represents the Self, which is the supreme non-dual Reality. The Self is known in four states, namely, the waking state, the dream state, the deep sleep state and the fourth state called the 'turīya'. All these states are represented in the three sounds of 'Om' (i.e. A, U, and M)[1] and the silence that follows and surrounds the syllable.

The sound 'A' represents the waking state; the sound 'U' represents the dream state and the sound 'M' represents the deep sleep state. The waking state is superimposed on the 'A' sound because it is the first of the three states of consciousness and so is the sound 'A', the very first of the letters of the alphabet in all languages. The dream is but a view

[1] In Sanskrit the vowel 'O' is constitutionally diphthong, compounded of 'A' and 'U'. OM can also be written as 'AUM'.

within the mind of the impressions that had reflected on the surface of the mental lake during the waking state. Besides, the dream state occurs between the waking and the deep sleep state and comes second among the three states of consciousness. And so, 'U' being next to 'A' in order of sounds (and also it is between 'A' and 'M') it is treated as representing the dream state. On the 'M' sound of Om is superimposed the deep sleep state. The comparison between the last sound of the Om and sleep lies in that, it is the closing sound of the syllable, just as deep sleep is the final stage of the mind in rest. A short pregnant silence is inevitable between two successive sounds of Oms. On this silence is superimposed the idea of the 'fourth state' known as 'turīya'. This is the state of perfect bliss when the individual self recognises its identity with the Supreme.

In Om the sounds A, U and M are called mātrās or forms; there is also in AUM the common principle called the amātra-Om, that which signifies the thing in itself, running through and pervading the three-fold phenomena of waking, dream and deep sleep. The law of memory is that the rememberer and the experiencer must be one and the same individual, or else memory is impossible. So, as we can remember all our experiences in all the three different planes, there must necessarily be a single common factor which was a witness of all the happenings in all the three planes. There must be some entity within ourselves who is present in the waking world, who moves and illumines the dream, who is a distant observer in the deep sleep world, and yet who is not conditioned by any of these three realms. This entity conceived as the fourth state (turīya) is the real, the changeless, the intelligent principle.

The syllable 'Om' symbolises both the spheres: (a) the phenomenal, visible sphere of the 'jagat' wherein the manifestations of time and space appear and perish, and (b) the transcendent, timeless sphere of the imperishable being, which is beyond, yet one with it. Thus A, the 'waking state,' U, the 'dream', M, the 'deep sleep' and the . silence, 'turīya': all the four together comprise the totality of this manifestation of Ātman – Brahman as a syllable. Just as the sound M manifests itself, grows, becomes transformed in its vocal quality and finally subsides into the silence that follows[1], so too the three 'states' or 'components of being', ultimately merge into the homogeneous silence of the 'fourth' (turīya). The other three states are transformations of the one experience, which taken together, constitute the totality of its modes, whether regarded from the microcosmic or from the macrocosmic point of view.

The A and U are as essential to the sound as M, or as the silence (turīya) against which the sound appears. Moreover it would be a mistake to say that AUM did not exist while silence reigned; for it would be still potentially present even in the silence. The actual manifestation of the syllable on the other hand is fleeting and evanescent, whereas the silence abides. The silence, indeed, is present elsewhere during a local pronunciation of Aum – that is to say (by analogy) transcendentally during the creation, manifestation and dissolution of the universe.

It may be asked as to why this particular word Om should be chosen as the word representative

[1] Which must be regarded as forming part of its sound in a latent, meaningful state of repose.

of the 'thought', out of which the universe has become manifested. The answer may be given in Svāmī Vivekananda's own words:

"This Om is the only possible symbol which covers the whole ground, and there is none other like it. The sphoṭa is the material of all words, yet it is not any definite word in its fully formed state. That is to say, if all the particularities which distinguish one word from another be removed, then what remains will be the sphoṭa. Therefore, this sphoṭa, is called the Nāda-Brahman, the Sound-Brahman. Now every word-symbol intended to express the inexpressible sphoṭa, will so particularise it, that it will no longer be the sphoṭa. That which particularises it the least and at the same time most approximately expresses its nature, will be the truest symbol thereof; and this is Om and the Om only; because, these three letters A, U, M pronounced in combination as Om can alone be the generalised symbol of all possible sounds. The letter 'A' is the least differentiate of all sounds. Again, all articulate sounds are produced in the space within the mouth – beginning with the root of the tongue and ending at the lips – the throat-sound is 'A' and 'M' is the last lip-sound; and 'U' exactly represents the rolling forward of the impulse which begins at the root of the tongue, continuing till it ends in the lips."

"If properly pronounced, this Om will represent in itself the whole phenomenon of sound production, and no other word can do this; and this, therefore, is the fittest symbol of the sphoṭa, which is the real meaning of the Om. And as the symbol can never be separated from the thing signified, the Om and the sphoṭa are one. And as the sphoṭa, being the finer side of the manifested universe, is nearer to God, and is indeed the first manifestation of divine Wisdom, this 'Om' is truly symbolic of God."

'Om' thus represents the entire manifested world and the unmanifest, and also that which lies beyond both the manifest and the unmanifest – the Brahman, which is the changeless substratum for the changing objects of the world of experiences.

To every mantra, 'Om', the praṇava, is added on. And without 'Om' no sacred-chant has its power. Just as a living body has no vitality when the life-giving breath is not flowing through its veins, so too a mantra has no life in it without the addition of the praṇava.

Students of Vedānta generally practise the repetition of and meditation upon the symbol provided by the praṇava. This is called as praṇava upāsanā.

'Om' represents in its silent significance, both the manifest and the unmanifest, which together constitute the entire gross and the subtle world. This word loka in Sanskrit is generally translated as 'world', but in its etymological meaning it signifies 'a field of experience'.

The entire possibility of experience in life has been terraced by the ṛṣis into fourteen worlds: seven higher lokas and seven lower worlds. There are three worlds in which a limited ego-centre comes to play its game of reincarnation and repeated deaths. These are: (i) Bhū-loka, the physical earth; (ii) Bhuvar-loka, the world next to the physical and closely connected with it, but constituted of finer matter, and (iii) Suvar-loka, has heavenly world.

Beyond these are the four other worlds wherein the ego comes to move about and enjoy in its higher evolutionary life, and they are called the Mahar-loka, Janaḥ-loka, Tapaḥ-loka and Satya-loka.

In the Hindu literature, we also find conceptions of other worlds as: Indra-loka, Candra-loka, Sūrya-loka, Pitṛ-loka and so on, which are special 'realms of experiences' located within the above regions.

Below these seven worlds, there is yet another set of seven worlds called the talas. They are named as Pā-tālam, Rasā-talam. Tala-talam. Su-talam. Vi-talam., and A-talam.

Of these fourteen 'worlds', Bhur-Bhuvaḥ-Svaḥ denoting the 'three worlds', are called the vyahṛtis. In the Gāyatrī mantra when these vyāhṛtis are chanted, the meditator can ṿisualise the 'three worlds' as arising from, existing in and disappearing into AUM. He can subjectively identify them with the waking, dream and deep sleep conditions of consciousness, transcending which extends the realm of the Infinite. All of them are represented in the symbol Om. In this sense, the vyahṛtis in the Gāyatrī represent in one sweep the 'entire world' of the subjective and objective experiences of man.

The Gāyatrī Mantra

"Om Bhūḥ – Bhuvaḥ – Suvaḥ
Om Tat – Savitur – Vareṇyam
Bhargo Devasya Dhīmahi
Dhiyo Yo Naḥ Pracodayāt"

The Hindu concept that the Gāyatrī mantra was declared at first by the Creator Himself, at the very beginning of creation, may be considered as an overexaggeration which is an unavoidable feature in many portions of the Vaidika literature. But it is also a fact that even the western scholars, who have been accepted by all as having a better historical sense, have themselves declared the Gāyatrī mantra as one of the oldest available divine hymns. And it is true that many revolutionary changes have taken place in our religious belief, and yet this mantra continues to persist and has even today a compelling charm of its own to millions of Hindu hearts. It is not only believed, but it has been actually observed, that by the repetition of this mantra with the right understanding of its sacred meaning, the ordinary negative tendencies in a human mind can be erased out to a large extent.

This mantra is never chanted for the purposes of material gains, physical or otherwise. Its very invocation concludes with an appeal to the pure consciousness to illumine more our heart – that is to say, it is a prayer unto the Self to unveil Itself and come to manifest as pure wisdom in our life.

Gāyatrī mantra is otherwise called Sāvitrī mantra. In the ancient literature of Vedānta, this mantra was indicated familiarly as Sāvitrī and this term has been given to Gāyatrī because it is dedicated to the deity called Savitṛ. In some rare old books, we find this mantra titled as Sāvitrī-Gāyatrī; it only means that it is an invocation dedicated to Lord Sun couched in the metre called Gāyatrī. This is considered to be the most important Vaidika mantra, written out in this metre and, therefore, by tradition this mantra has come to be known as Gāyatrī.

The Gāyatrī metre is generally constituted of three lines of eight syllables each. The three lines of Gāyatrī-Sāvitrī mantra are as follows[1]:

"..............................

Om Tat - Savitur- Vareṇyam

Bhargo Devasya Dhīmahi

DhiyoYo Naḥ Pracodayāt

You will find in the above that the first line has only seven syllables. This is explained generally in two ways: (a)the syllable 'ṇyam' is constituted of 'ṇi' plus 'am' and, therefore, there are the required eight letters in the line, and (b) that the line is to be read along with Omkāra which would supply the missing syllable. The former is the idea of Śrī Śaṅkarācārya. In his commentary on *Bṛhadāraṇyaka-upaniṣad,* Śaṅkara splits the letter 'ṇyam' into its two component parts and considers that the rules of the metre are thereby fully obeyed.

The seer of the mantra is the royal sage Viśvāmitra. All the mantras belonging to the third maṇḍala of the *Ṛg-veda* are attributed to sage

[1] Gāyatrī mantra belongs to the *Ṛg-veda,* and it is found in the third maṇḍala, in its sixtieth sūtra as the tenth mantra.

Viśvāmitra. The Gāyatrī mantra is also seen in the *Śukla Yajur-veda and Kṛṣṇa Yajur-veda.*

This mantra is dedicated to the Lord Savitṛ. That Savitṛ represents Lord Sun is the accepted version even though there are some scholars who protest against this. The Sun gives all illumination to the world and any prayer for light should certainly be addressed to 'the source of all light' in the material world – the sun. In the *Gītā* the Lord says, 'The light that pervades the sun and the moon is all His light. Thus Savitṛ, the Lord of Gāyatrī is nothing other than the light of Consciousness, the Infinite, the Absolute.

"..............................

Om Tat - Savitur - Vareṇyam

Bhargo Devasya Dhīmahi

Dhiyo Yo Naḥ Pracodayāt"

which means : -

'We meditate upon the auspicious godly light of the Lord Sun; may that heavenly light illumine our thought flow in our intellect.' This mantra is always chanted along with praṇava and the vyāhṛtis.

The usual prescribed daily worship (sandhyā karma) of a Hindu mainly included repetition of this Gāyatrī mantra. In the ancient days, sandhyā vandanā, the daily prayer, was only a purificatory act, it is only a method of reintegrating one's own mind that has run wild during the day and has drowned completely in total inertia in the night.

In *Manusmṛti*[1] we read: 'In the early dawn by doing this japa standing, one ends all sins committed during the night and by doing this japa in the evening by sitting, one ends one's sins committed during the day.' Sin here means, as everywhere else in our sacred books, the agitations created in our mental life by our own negative actions and the tendency to repeat the same, which is left by them as impressions upon the mind.

It is only afterwards, the importance of Gāyatrī grew to its present status. Later on, sometime during our steady slipping into our present decadent state, the belief that Gāyatrī cannot be chanted without the sacred thread became much rampant; a belief which we seldom meet with in the ancient lore. When we are thus daily using this mantra in our worship, it is chanted along with the

---

[1] *Manusmṛti*-102

praṇava and the vyāhṛtis. We may or may not add the praṇava to the second line:

"..

"Om Bhūḥ- Bhuvaḥ-Suvaḥ

Om Tat - Savitur - Vareṇyam

Bhargo Devasya Dhīmahī

Dhiyo Yo Naḥ Pracodayāt"

There are two sandhyās in a day. The term 'sandhyā' means the blending point of day and night. In the ancient literature we fail to find any importance for the mid-day worship. According to the literature of Vedānta, the ṛṣis seem to insist only upon the morning and evening prayers. This mid-day prayer might have filtered into our creed, perhaps, as an unnecessary borrowing from the Mohammedan cult. Early morning when the east blushes in light and in the evening when the golden light fades into darkness we have the two sandhyās. Generally, the morning prayers are done most profitably between 4-30 a.m. and 5 a.m. which is called the Brāhma-muhūrta; and in the evening the interval between 6 p.m. and 7 p.m.[1] is the sacred hour for the evening prayers.

[1] 'First show film time' of the modern man is the perfect sandhyā for the seekers, even in our own time.

In *Manusmṛti* we find very interesting and clear directions on these prayers and worship.

'Afterwards getting up from bed, after answering the calls of nature, purifying yourself completely, disallowing the mind to wander hither and thither, sincerely perform the morning japa standing on your feet and repeating the mantra very very slowly.'[1] Elsewhere we also read, 'In the morning worship till the sun rises above the horizon do the japa standing and in the evening worship sitting down do your japa until the stars emerge out.'

In the ancient days,· the daily worship (sandhyā karma) was not so elaborate as they have become now, after the days of the sūtras and āgamas. In the beginning, the Veda advises us to sing the Gāyatrī mantra both at the dawn and at the dusk standing in water facing the Sun – naturally, in the morning the face will be eastward turned; and in the evening the face will be westward turned. The one who is chanting the mantra is to carry water in his folded palm and at the end of each mantra japa, he must offer

[1] *Manusmṛti*-2/101

that water to the Lord. This is called the offerings unto the Great Guest (arghya pradāna).

As this water in his folded palm is offered, the devotee says: 'This Sun is Brahman' (āsāvādityo Brahma) and performs ātma pradakṣiṇā turning round himself by his right. This signifies a suggestion that the devotee is 'going round' in reverence and devotion around the Lord Sun, the Brahman which is the Self in himself.

The Gāyatrī is chanted generally at each sandhyā, a minimum of ten times. However, according to one's faith, convenience and devotion one can chant any number of times in any sandhyā. But never is this mantra chanted at night; after the sunset Gāyatrī should not be repeated, is the rule.

In Taittirīya āraṇyaka[1] we have in a story form a glorious explanation of the why of this daily chanting of Gāyatrī and the offering of arghya poured towards the sun. The story is a typical example of the Vaidika style of mysticism.

[1] Āraṇyaka is the upāsanā kāṇḍa in the Vedas – the portion that connects the purely ritualistic section called the Brāhmaṇa with the essentially philosophic portion, called the Upaniṣads.

While describing a story, it is made to convey a deep significance in our subjective life itself.

In an island called Aruṇam a tribe of devils called Manadehas live, and so their native island is also called as Man-Deha Aruṇam. These devils every day morning, in hoards, conquer space and reach almost near the sun threatening to destroy Him, when the water thrown by the Gāyatrī japists becomes lightning strong and the devils get struck by that and retreat into their own island. This happens daily.

The story as such would read silly, but so too the European music page books for me! But when a man renders it eloquently upon his musical instruments, the silly page melts into a torrential outpour of harmony and rhythm.

Mind (mana) and body (deha) are the sources of our activities[1] and they, with their likes and dislikes, their emotions and appetites, their passions and cravings bring out from us a host of passionate animal instincts which try to conquer and destroy the spiritual essence in us, the Brahman, the Sun in us. The essential brilliance of the human intellect

[1] Hence the name of the island as Mana-deha.

thus gets clouded by the approaching hosts of these passions and Gāyatrī japa and its consequent effects are thunder and lightning descending down upon them!!!

Thousands of years after the Vedas, we got the sūtras and the authors of each of them one by one recommended more and more items to be incorporated in the daily worship. Following the sūtras, after a time, the āgamas came to be written and their authors had their own contributions to make to the general form of our daily worship. Āgamas mainly describe the ritualistic regulations and the rules in worshipping Viṣṇu. Śiva and Śakti. Each āgama claimed the Gāyatrī as its own and they declared that Gāyatrī is presided over by Viṣṇu or Śiva or Śakti according to the name of the Lord that is recommended by the āgama.

The Śāktas gave the idea that Gāyatrī is the infinite Goddess and made her a feminine deity. Gāyatrī Devi soon became the mother of the Vedas. And even nowadays it is very freely believed by brāhmaṇas that if they have chanted Gāyatrī they have chanted the Vedas.

Very many interesting and irrational, though quite effective, beliefs have come round the Gāyatrī mantra and its efficacy. For[1] anyone frightened in the dark, immediately Gāyatrī mantra chanting is advised to get over the nervousness of his fright· If anyone had some such delusory fright as a result of which the individual is prostrate with illness, then some brāhmaṇa priests of true devotion and pure moral life are engaged in conducting a congregational japa by the bed-side of the patient.

These beliefs only prove that the very name of the mantra is fully justified. The term Gāyatrī itself means[2] 'That mantra which protects him who chants it.' It is also believed in India that on starting for any important and great work if a man detects some bad omen, he must immediately sit down and chant eleven times the Gāyatrī. If, on starting again, he meets with a new set of bad omens, he is to sit down again and chant Gāyatrī

[1] Personally I do not believe in these – but I am reporting here that those who are suffering from these mental weaknesses can find a consolation and true remedy by repeating Gāyatrī mantra.

[2] Gāyantaṁ trāyate iti Gāyatrī.

for sixteen times. These will remove the effects of the bad omens encountered, is yet another belief.

In India, a Hindu boy is initiated into the Gāyatrī mantra very early in his life. This is done during a social ritual called the upanayana ceremony, presided over, by the head of the family and family priest. In the literature of Vedānta we find mention of the Gāyatrī dīkṣā. The term dīkṣā means a discipline which one must undergo in order that one may become fit for taking part in any Vaidika ritual. The word upanayana means 'bringing near' – bringing preceptor who initiates the boy by giving him the sacred Gāyatrī mantra. It is interesting to note that there are definite prescriptions ordering the age at which the boys are to be initiated. Manu[1] gives the age as five for a brāhmaṇa, as six for kṣatriya and eight for a vaiśya; the maximum ages at which initiation may be given are at 16, 22 and 24 respectively.

The Vaidika declarations glorify this initiation and insist that life after Gāyatrī-dīkṣā is almost a second birth, since in this ritualism the boy is initiated into a new transformation in his subtle life.

---

[1] *Manusmṛti* 37-38

'The father and mother have given birth to him from mutual desire, so that he is born from the womb; let this be known as his physical birth.'

'But that birth which is given, according to the ordinance, through the Sāvitrī, by the preceptor who has mastered the Vedas, that is the true birth, the unaging and immortal.'[1]

After this initiation the boy is considered as twice born (dvija).

The full Gāyatrī mantra has got, in fact, a fourth line also[2] which invokes that which lies beyond the effulgence, and it asserts in an intimate subjective experience of the devotee, his identity with it, as 'that is this'. The fourth line is mentioned in *Chāndogya, Bṛhadāraṇyaka* and *Brahmasūtra*. This line has been always preserved as very sacred and secret, and it is only given out to full time seekers or to self dedicated sannyāsins. This line is not so much for chanting as for experiencing in the highest moments of intense meditation in samādhi.

---

[1] *Manusmṛti* II-147-148

[2] 'Paro Rajase: Savad - Om'–meaning. He who is transcending the effulgence is this'.

In the ancient days, the ladies used to chant Gāyatrī as freely as men. So says Manu. In the ancient days all ladies had their upanayana performed. They used to learn the Vedas, teach the Vedas to others and chant the Gāyatrī mantra. Here the term 'ladies' used cannot, by any stretch of imagination, be conceived as meaning only the ladies of the brāhmaṇa or the kṣatriya families.

In fact, spiritual unfoldment through mantra upāsanā is found more readily in ladies than in gentlemen, because the former have not got the nerve shattering personal contacts with the competitive problems of life. Thus the śāstra injunctions and our own personal observations take us to the conclusion that women too can, rather should, chant the Gāyatrī mantra regularly in their morning and evening worship.

In fact, there are repeated declarations in our Hindu sacred books that if the effects of the sādhanā performed by men are their own, the spiritual benefits acquired by the women folk are shared by their husbands, children, their families and the entire society.

The deeper philosophic import of Gāyatrī is very clear. The mantra as it stands obviously invokes the Lord Sun and pleads to Him to illumine the intellect of the seeker. The sunlight cannot, it is certain, illumine the intellect in us... the white and the grey matter of the brain!!!

In our inner life, the sun represents, the light giver, the illuminator of all experiences, the Ātman. This pure Consciousness in us, the inner centre of our personality, around which the matter envelopments function with mathematical precision ...just as around the sun, the centre of the universe, the entire solar system revolves, each planet and star at its appointed speed and each along its appointed path... is being invoked to shine more and more in our intellect.

If the sun were not there, life would have been impossible. Without the Ātman the matter envelopments would become inert and dead.

When this inner sun of life is appealed to for illumining the intellect better, it reads as an absurd paradox. The infinite light of Wisdom, the supreme Self, is never contaminated in its eternal effulgence. It is ever the same. Its intensity cannot increase or decrease.

Therefore, all that the devotee means is, 'may my intellect be steady without agitations; may it be clean without the dirt of passions. May the light of consciousness come to shine forth a brilliant beam of its radiance through my intellect.' Thus may my perception of the world be clear, my discrimination subtle, my judgements correct and quick, my comprehension of situations and beings precise and wise.

A Note From Gurudev

By a sheer accident I came across a very old book, title pages all defaced, in the hands of a brāhmaṇa in Devaprayāga, and in it saw Śrī Ādi Śaṅkara's own annotations upon the Gāyatrī mantra.

I am sure it is a rare find and therefore, I give here the original with a free rendering in English. I hope it will be useful to all spiritual students and seekers walking the path of meditation.

Chinmaya

Word meaning of Gāyatrī

गायत्री शुद्धा प्रत्यग्ब्रह्मैक्यबोधिका ॥

gāyatrī śuddhā pratyagbrahmaikyabodhikā.

गायत्री – gāyatrī; शुद्धा – pure; प्रत्यक् – individual Self; ब्रह्म – Brahman; ऐक्य – oneness; बोधिका – indicates

Gāyatrī mantra indicates the knowledge of the essential oneness of the Self in each one of us and the Self everywhere.

सर्वबुद्धि-संज्ञान्तःकरण प्रकाशकः
सर्वसाक्षी प्रत्यगात्मा इति उच्यते ॥

sarvabuddhi-sañjñāntaḥkaraṇa prakāśakaḥ
sarvasākṣī pratyagātmā iti ucyate.

सर्व-बुद्धि – all intellects; संज्ञः – knower; अन्तःकरणः – inner equipment; प्रकाशकः – illuminator; सर्व-साक्षी – witness of all; प्रत्यग्-आत्मा – the Self in everyone; इति – thus; उच्यते – is said

The knower of all the intellects that is the

illuminator of all the thoughts and in all intellects, a witness of all the intellects, the essential Self is indicated (by the Gāyatrī Mantra)

तस्य प्रचोदयात् शब्दनिष्ठस्य आत्मनः स्वरूपभूतं परं ब्रह्म-तत्सवितुरित्यादि पदैः निर्दिश्यते ।

tasya pracodayāt śabdaniṣṭhasya ātmanaḥ svarūpabhūtaṁ paraṁ brahma-tatsaviturityādi padaiḥ nirdiśyate.

तस्य – that (supreme Brahman); प्रचोदयात् – inspires; शब्द-निष्ठस्य – abiding in that sound; आत्मनः – of supreme Brahman; स्वरूप-भूतम् – indicator of the Self; परम् ब्रह्म – supreme Brahman (Reality); तत् – that (para Brahman); सवितुः – Sun (Gāyatrī); इत्यादि – and so on; पदैः – words; निर्दिश्यते – indicates

The supreme Brahman (the ultimate, transcendental Reality) alone is the Self, invoking whom the prayer 'inspire us' was raised. This Self is indicated in the Gāyatrī mantra by the term Sun (सवितुः) and so on.

अत्र तत्-शब्देन प्रत्यग्भूतं स्वतःसिद्धं परं ब्रह्म उच्यते ॥

atra tat-śabdena pratyagbhūtaṁ svataḥsiddhaṁ paraṁ brahma ucyate.

अत्र – thus; तत् – that (indicates unmanifest); शब्देन – by the words; प्रत्यग्-भूतम् – self-evident; स्वतःसिद्धम् – Self-illuminator; परम् ब्रह्म – param Brahman (supreme Reality); उच्यते – is said

Here the word 'That' (तत्) indicates the self-evident, Self-within, which is nothing but the Self-in-all, the Supreme Self.

सवितुः इति सृष्टिस्थितिलय-लक्षणस्य सर्व प्रपंचस्य द्वैतभावस्य अधिष्ठानं लक्ष्यते ॥

savituḥ iti sṛṣṭisthitilaya-lakṣaṇasya sarva prapañcasya dvaitabhāvasya adhiṣṭhānaṁ lakṣyate.

सवितुः इति – the Sun; सृष्टि-स्थिति-लय – creation, sustenance and destruction; लक्षणस्य – characteristics; सर्व प्रपंचस्य – of the entire universe; द्वैत-भावस्य – of the nature of duality; अधिष्ठानम् – substratum; लक्ष्यते – is indicated

The term 'Sun' (सवितुः) indicates the One substratum for all the delusory experiences of plurality and their illusory play in a field of creation, sustenance and destruction.

वरेण्यम् - इति सर्ववरेणीयं निरतिशयानन्दरूपम् ॥

vareṇyam–itisarvavareṇīyaṁniratiśayānandarūpam.

वरेण्यम्-इति – adorable; सर्व-वरेणीयम् – courted by all; निरतिशय आनन्द-स्वरूपम् – of the nature of infinite Bliss

Worshipful, adorable, (वरेण्यम्) means 'That which is courted by all' as It is of the nature of infinite Bliss.

During Japa (जपकाले), the term vareṇyam (वरेण्यम्) should be pronounced as vareṇīyaṁ (वरेणीयम्).

भर्ग - इति अविद्यादिदोषभर्जनात्मक ज्ञानैकविषयत्वात् ।

bhargaḥ – iti avidyādidoṣabharjanātmaka jñānaikaviṣayatvāt,

भर्ग-इति – resplendant; अविद्या आदि – ignorance and so on; दोषः – misapprehension (imperfection); भर्जनात्मक – destroyer; ज्ञान – jñāna; ऐक-विषयत्वात् – the principal subject

Resplendent (भर्गः) here is indicative of the knowledge which will destroy all imperfections (misapprehensions) projected by ignorance (अविद्या – non-apprehension of Reality). Where ignorance (veiling of Reality – तमस्) and its consequent results of misapprehension (agitations विक्षेप – रजस्) are destroyed, the apprehension of Reality becomes self-evident and immediate.

देवस्य – इति सर्वद्योतनात्मक-अखण्डचिदेकरसम् ॥

devasya–itisarvadyotanātmaka-akhaṇḍacidekarasam.

देवस्य इति – self-shining; सर्व – all – both inside and outside; द्योतनात्मकः – self illuminator; एक-रसम् – uniform; अखण्ड – without any break; चित् – pure Conciousness

The Light (देवस्य) here suggests the ever-present pure Consciousness, illumining everything within and without, in all the three states – waking, dream and deep sleep.

सवितुर्देवस्य इत्यत्र षष्ठयर्थी राहोः शिरोवद्
औपचारिकः बुद्ध्यादि सर्वदृश्यस्य साक्षिलक्षणम् ॥

saviturdevasya ityatra ṣaṣṭhyarthī rāhoḥ śirovad
aupacārikaḥ buddhyādi sarvadṛśyasya sākṣilakṣaṇam.

सवितुः – of the Sun; देवस्य – light (conciousness of Self); इत्यत्र – here; षष्ठी अर्थी – in the sense of genitive case; राहोः शिर – head of the Rāhu; वत् – like; औपचारिकः – without any particular meaning; बुद्धि-आदि – intellect and so on; सर्व दृश्यस्य – of all that is seen; साक्षि-लक्षणम् – characteristics of a witness

The terms 'Sun' (सवितु) and 'light' (देवस्य) are used here in a construction meaning 'Sun's light' – the 'consciousness of the Self.' The genitive care (षष्ठी विभक्तिः) employed here is to be considered as a redundancy just as in saying the 'head of Rāhu.' (Rāhu has only head; but when you say 'head of Rāhu it can create a misconception in our mind that Rāhu has a body separately.) Thus when we say the 'light of Consciousness' or the 'light of Self' the Self is not to be understood as anything other than consciousness, the Light within. It only means that the Self is the 'witness' of all activities of the intellect and all such other equipments.

यन्मे स्वरूपं तत् सर्वाधिष्ठानरूपं परमानन्दम् ।
निरस्तसमस्तानर्थरूपं स्वप्रकाशचिदात्मकं ब्रह्म इत्येवम् ॥

yanme svarūpaṁ tat sarvādhiṣṭhānarūpaṁ paramānandam,
nirastasamastānartharūpaṁ svaprakāśacidātmakaṁ brahma ityevam.

यत् – which; मे – my, mine; स्वरूपम् – real nature; तत् – that; सर्व अधिष्ठान – substratum for all; रूपम् – nature; परम् आनन्दम् – supreme Bliss; निरस्त – destroyer; समस्त – all; अनर्थ – calamity; रूपम् – nature; स्वप्रकाश – Self-effulgent; चिदात्मकम् – pure Consciousness; ब्रह्म – Brahman; इति एवम् – alone is

That which is my own 'real nature', my own Self is nothing but the supreme Bliss, the substratum for all, beyond all sorrows and tragedies, self-effulgent, pure Consciousness, the Brahman alone.

धीमहि - ध्यायेम

dhīmahi - dhyāyema

धीमहि – *dhīmahi*; ध्यायेम – *dhyāyema* – we meditate

The term *'dhīmahi'* (धीमहि) is the Vaidika construction for 'we meditate' (ध्यायेम).

एवं सति प्रत्यगात्मनः ब्रह्मणा सह तादात्म्यरूपमेकत्वं भवति ।

evaṁ sati pratyagātmanaḥ brahmaṇā saha tādātmyarūpamekatvaṁ bhavati,

एवम् – thus; सति – in circumstances; प्रत्यग्-आत्मनः – Self within; ब्रह्मणा सह – with Brahman; तादात्म्य

रूपम् – identical nature; एकत्वम् – oneness; भवति – becomes

Thus a perfect oneness of the individual Self (प्रत्यगात्मनः) with the Self of all (ब्रह्मणा) is established.

तया सर्वात्मकब्रह्मबोधकोऽयं गायत्रीमन्त्रः संपद्यते ।

tayā sarvātmakabrahmabodhako'yaṁ gāyatrīmantraḥ sampadyate,

तया – therefore; सर्वात्मकः – omnipresent; ब्रह्म बोधकः – indicator of Brahman; अयम् – this; गायत्री मन्त्रः – Gāyatrī mantra; संपद्यते – becomes

Now it is clear that the Gāyatrī mantra indicates in its deeper meaning the invocation of the supreme Self, which is the one life everywhere that enlivens all creatures.

अथ सप्तव्याहृतीनां अयमर्थः

atha saptavyāhṛtīnām ayamarthaḥ

अथ – now; सप्त – seven; व्याहृतीनाम् – vyāhṛtis; अयम् – this; अर्थः – is the meaning

In the Vaidika vocabulary Bhuḥ (भूः), Bhuvaḥ (भूवः) Svaḥ (स्वः), Mahaḥ (महः) Janaḥ (जनः) Tapaḥ (तपः) Satyam (सत्यम) altogether seven in number are called as the 'vyāhṛtis' (व्याहृतयः). Of the seven, only the first three are invoked in routine chanting of the Gāyatrī mantra. All of them are indicative of the infinite eternal Brahman.

भूः इति नित्यत्वं उच्यते - तथा हि सर्वव्यापि सर्वकालिकं सर्वोत्कृष्टं नित्यमुक्तं आत्मस्वरूपं सन्मात्र उच्यते ॥

bhūḥ iti nityatvam ucyate - tathā hi sarvavyāpi sarvakālikaṁ
sarvotkṛṣṭaṁ nityamuktaṁ ātmasvarūpaṁ sanmātra ucyate.

भूः इति नित्यत्वम् – bhūḥ and so on which means permanent; उच्यते – is said; तथा हि – in addition to that; सर्व-व्यापि – all-pervading; सर्व-कालिकम् – which exists in all the three periods of time; सर्व उत्कृष्टम् – the best of all; नित्य मुक्तम् – ever liberated; आत्म-स्वरूपम् – of the nature of one's own Self; सत्-मात्र – Truth and truth alone; उच्यते – is said to be (invoked)

Bhūḥ (भूः) indicates the permanent. The all-pervading One that exists at all periods of time, the most auspicious, ever free Self, of the nature of pure existence in all forms is invoked by this term.

भुवः - इति सर्वं भावयति प्रकाशयति इति
व्युत्पत्त्या चिद्रूपत्वं उच्यते ॥

bhuvaḥ – iti sarvaṁ bhāvayati prakāśayati iti vyutpattyā cidrūpatvam ucyate.

भुवः-इति – The term Bhuvaḥ; सर्वम् भावयति प्रकाशयति – imagines, illuminates all beings (Viśva – jagat); इति – thus; व्युत्पत्ति – etymology; चिद् रूपत्वम् – of the nature of pure Consciousness; उच्यते – is suggested (said to be)

The term Bhuvaḥ (भुवः) suggests the pure Consciousness according to the etymology of the term: Bhuvaḥ comes from 'imagines' (भावयति) suggesting the awareness that illumines (प्रकाशयति) our thoughts.

स्वः - इति सुष्टु सर्वैः व्रियमाणस्वरूपं उच्यते ॥

svaḥ – iti suṣṭu sarveḥ vriyamāṇasvarūpaṁ ucyate.

स्वः-इति – the term svaḥ; सुष्टु – well; सर्वैं – by all;

ध्रियमाण स्वरूपम् – courted ardently by all; स्वरूपम् – our own Self; उच्यते – said to be

Svaḥ (स्वः) as a vyāhṛti in its import suggests 'one's own essential reality', because what is courted ardently (ध्रियमाण) very much (सुष्ठु) by all (सर्वैः) is our own Self.

महः-इति महीयते पूज्यते व्युत्पत्त्या सर्वातिशयत्वं उच्यते ॥

mahaḥ-iti mahīyate pūjyate vyutpattyā sarvātiśayatvam ucyate.

महः-इति – the term mahaḥ suggests; महीयते – glorious; पूज्यते – worshipful; इति व्युत्पत्त्या – by this etymology; सर्वैः – by all; अतिशयत्वम् – most glorious; उच्यते – is said to be

The term Mahaḥ (महः) as it derives itself from 'glorious' (महीयते) meaning the 'worshipful' (पूज्यते) directly suggests the 'most glorious' or the 'most worshipful' which is the supreme Self.

जनः - इति जनयतीति व्युत्पत्त्या सकलकारणत्वं उच्यते ॥

janaḥ – iti janayatīti vyutpattyā sakalakāraṇatvam ucyate.

जनः-इति – the term Janaḥ suggests; जनयति-इति – he who creates; व्युत्पत्त्या – by etymology; सकल – all (entire universe); कारणत्वम् – cause; उच्यते – is said to be

The vyāhṛti Janaḥ (जनः) again, based upon its derivation from 'creates' (जनयति) suggests that which is the 'one cause' for all names and forms within and without.

तपः - इति सर्वतेजोरूपम् ॥

tapaḥ – iti sarvatejorūpam.

तपः-इति – the term Tapaḥ suggests; सर्व – all; तेज – Self-resplendant; रूपम् – of the nature

The term Tapaḥ (तपः) means resplendent splendrous, full of brilliancy. The Self as consciousness alone is the source of all light in the universe.

सत्यम्-इति सर्वबाधारहितम् ॥

satyam-iti sarvabādhārahitam.

सत्यम्-इति – the term Satyam suggests; सर्व बाधा – all obstacles; रहितम् – devoid of

Satyam (सत्यम्) – state which is beyond the pale of all limitations (such as sorrows and pains).

These seven vyāhṛtis are described as the seven 'worlds' (लोकाः). 'World' means 'field of experiences'.

Now:

एतदुक्तं भवति

etaduktaṁ bhavati

एतद् – this; उक्तम् भवति – is said by us

Therefore, we said in the beginning that Gāyatrī indicates the infinite Reality, the Brahman.

सद्रूपं तद् ओंकारवाच्यं ब्रह्मैव भूरादयाः सर्वे लोकाः
ओंकारवाच्य ब्रह्मात्मकाः न तद्व्यतिरिक्तं किंचिदस्ति ॥

sadrūpaṁ tad oṅkāravācyaṁ brahmaiva bhūrādayāḥ sarve lokāḥ
oṅkāravācya brahmātmakāḥ na tadvayatiriktaṁ kiñcidasti.

तद्-सद्-रूपम् – that pure existence; ओंकार-वाच्यम् – which is indicated by the Omkāra; ब्रह्म एव – is

Brahman alone; भूः आदयः – bhuḥ and so on; सर्वे लोकाः – all the seven worlds; ओंकार वाच्य – indicates through Omkāra; ब्रह्म आत्मकाः – Brahman alone; तद् व्यतिरिक्तम् – other than that (Supreme); किंचित् न अस्ति – there is nothing

The Self, which is pure existence, is the meaning indicated by the Vaidika mantra Om, signifying Brahman, bhuḥ and so on, all the seven worlds are also comprehended in Om-meaning and so Brahman alone is meant here and nothing other than It, in fact, ever exists.

इति व्याहृतयोऽपि सर्वात्मब्रह्मबोधिकाः ॥

iti vyāhṛtayo'pi sarvātmabrahmabodhikāḥ

इति – thus; व्याहृतय – the seven vyāhṛtis; अपि – too; सर्वात्म ब्रह्म बोधिकाः – suggestive of the Self in all is the Brahman

Thus, even all the seven vyāhṛtis (भू भुवः स्वः and so on) are also pointing out, with their suggestions, the Brahman, the Self in all.

Om Tat Sat